INTRODUCTION

Dad's Army has immortalised one unit of the Home Guard forever. Everyone in Britain, it seems, knows about the antics of the civilian army, led by Captain Mainwaring, which defended Walmington-on-Sea, a fictional village on Britain's south coast.

Based on Jimmy Perry's experiences as a seventeen-year-old in the LDV and Home Guard, the series was brought to the small screen with the help of David Croft and Michael Mills, head of comedy at the BBC. Eighty episodes over nine series and a healthy repeat rate have made *Dad's Army* one of the most popular comedies of all time.

This little booklet of *Home Guard Humour* shows that the japes and scrapes that the Walmington-on-Sea platoon got into were no different from that of any other unit of the Home Guard. First published in May 1945, in an edition of perhaps only a few thousand, *Home Guard Humour* was written by Home Guardists for Home Guardists. Using cartoons, the booklet takes us through the history of the Home Guard, from the early days with no weapons or uniforms to the disbanding of the largest civilian army ever formed in Britain. Few copies of *Home Guard Humour* have survived to the present day and it was a chance purchase for myself at an antique postcard fair in Woking. My interest in the Home Guard was sparked by *Dad's Army*, and by my grandfather's role in the Home Guard, and I recognise the humour within this booklet from his stories, as well as those of *Dad's Army* itself.

Seventy years after the founding of the Home Guard, it seems appropriate to republish *Home Guard Humour* and bring it to an audience who have grown up with *Dad's Army*. Enjoy the cartoons but don't forget to ask your grandfather before it is too late what he did in the war. You may be surprised!

Campbell McCutcheon,
August 2010

FOREWORD

HERE was an amazing response to the broadcast appeal of Mr Anthony Eden in May 1940. At that time Britain stood in dire peril, for the low countries were being over-run and France was on the verge of defeat. Dunkirk came and with it an increase in tension.

In this hour of urgent need – when we had but the shadow of an army – was born the LDV, later to become the Home Guard. Its appeal was instant and to it flocked many who brought with them the spirit of those distant years and with that spirit was entwined the immortal humour of the British under arms.

This booklet seeks to perpetuate some of that fun and will, we trust, be regarded as a permanent memento of momentous days.

THE FIRST PARADE!

Every section of the community responded to the call – drayman and director, lorryman and lord – all were there! Everyone was 'on the level', discipline was but a thread, but spirit was high. Memory could not easily recall the correct military thing to do or say – and there had been many changes in twenty-five years! This all led to amusing situations, but amid the lack of knowledge, there shone a humour, which somehow matched every circumstance and made light of every trial.

This humour was no modern attribute, born of the hour's need; it was in the same rich vein as that of Agincourt or Arras; it was the traditional British type, with just the appropriate up-to-date words where necessary. The vocabulary, however, was always complete and never hesitant.

Early on, the regions on the coast received an issue of denims, but for the most part the many variants of civilian attire continued for some time to provide astounding contrasts of colour and cut on early parades. Khaki armbands were issued, printed L.D.V. in bold letters, yet even these were in short supply; there were by no means enough to go round. Indeed, when patrols returned from

THE ARMBAND

some dark pilgrimage, it was strictly laid down that the armbands should be handed over to the outgoing group. And often wordy warfare would ensue if someone tried to purloin one!

Firearms were an assorted array and included shot-guns, privately loaned. Some of these were of beautiful design and workmanship and were evidently treasured possessions of the owners. Revolvers too of ancient vintage came out from the dusty debris of the last war.

Some made their own lethal tools, which were of wonderful construction and ingenuity. One of these was called the 'cheese-cutter'. It was a piece of piano wire with handles at either end. The dark design was to creep up behind the enemy, sweep the wire over his head and round his neck, change hands on the handles and pull until – as one instructor put it – 'the wire comes straight again in y'hands again.'

Who will fail to remember the first drills? With a shock, the 'old hands' learned that forming fours was no longer practised. Instead, 'threes' was the correct

BEDS

— AND BEDLAM

ISSUING BATTLE DRESS

formation. Even this radical change did not, however, cause much concern, but to those who had, in the long ago, 'numbered off' with a deafening shout into a neighbour's ear, it was now a tame thing to line up on the markers.

Apart from the nightly patrols and guard duties, another important job had to be done; this was that of assisting the police in checking identities in the traffic of the roads. It was no uncommon sight to see one or two L.D.V. men carefully scrutinizing the identity card of a livid lorry driver, who had lined up behind him a long collection of every conceivable type of transport. Sometimes the sight of a rifle, or shot gun or revolver brought quaking fear to the over-sensitive, especially if identity cards had been mislaid or left at home.

The guarding of important buildings, bridges, etc., meant long vigils by night, but the job was done with a blithe spirit and much conversation, usually upon the course of the war. This latter was nearly always settled before the Relief came. Unfortunately, Hitler did not seem to heed the logic poured out Foolishly, he continued the war.

THE MOBILE SECTION !

WITH THE GREASE OF YEARS UPON THEM

Patrols were organised to traverse the open spaces – in case paratroopers might decide to drop on them. Many miles were walked by small groups intent upon the job, what-time in the distance the rumble of anti-aircraft guns and shell-burst could be heard, while the sky twinkled with flashes and was lit by flares. False alarms there were, too! And how eagerly the fellows turned out, hoping for a slice of excitement!

There were primitive beds at the temporary HQ's, beds intimately reminiscent of the last war – just wire-mesh and a few blankets. But, after the keen air of the night, even these poor imitations of the home bed were welcome receptacles of a tired body – tired, perhaps, long before Home Guard duties began.

The digging of trenches and sand-bagging were early and arduous efforts. It was illuminating to observe how the manual worker triumphed over his softer-skinned comrades. Blistered fingers, however, did not deter, though often there was some banter on 'who could take it'.

Every important road in the country had road blocks upon it somewhere. Often these were merely sand-bag edifices, allowing but a small space for the passage of a lorry – and the driver thereof became unusually eloquent if he could spot a group of L.D.V.'s, whom he regarded as the perpetrators of his troubles.

The national issue of denims satisfied the eager desire to have a uniform. Local tailors had a full time altering some suits, but others remained on the wearer, touching the salient parts of the body.

ON GUARD

ROUTE MARCH

THE NEW PIP

When real khaki was issued, the volunteers (now designated, at the request of the Prime Minister, the Home Guard) looked more like a military force, even though there were many rotund waistlines, while some belts strained grimly at the last hole! Army boots, too, gave a clatter which conveyed the impression that military men were afoot. But the leather gaiters! Somehow, these rigid things never quite reconciled themselves to Home Guard shins. Later, they were replaced by ones made of canvas – to everybody's delight.

In these early days there was no actual chain of command handing down its orders. Organisation was rather simple and – owing to the stress of the times – a trifle loose. Later there was considerable re-organisation – then more re-organisation; in fact, the whole period of the existence of the Home Guard was a sequence or re-organisations! This provided ample opportunity for acid, and even rude, comment by the 're-organised', but they went through with it, grousing at each change-over, but accepting it in great good part.

THE STICKY BOMB

THE NIGHT PATROL

One of the results of full military status was the appointment of regular adjutants, training officers and quarter-masters. They came – and with them a great increase in form-filling and correspondence. Indeed, the returns that had to be made by them to the 'higher-ups' were really a full-time job. No trio in 'regular' employment could have been harder worked than those the Army seconded to Home Guard units.

Perhaps the quartermaster had the biggest worry. His position in any army and in any age was always a trial. Certainly the part-time quasi-civilian Home Guards did not require any coaching in the gentle art of scrounging! They were as good as any Regulars after an understandable hesitance at the beginning of things.

ON THE RANGE

In addition, regular P.S.I.'s were posted. These brought to the Home Guard their powers of instruction in weapons and also the correct use of the parade-ground voice. Most N.C.O.'s, however, could be relied upon to produce the appropriate volume when the occasion demanded it.

Ranks, corresponding to those of the Regular Army, came along, even to the inflictions of sergeants and sergeants-major. Pips replaced blue bars on epaulets. Gradually the Home Guard sorted itself out – in sections, platoons, companies and battalions. It went into strict training with rifles, newly arrived from the USA, with the grease of years upon them.

To the 'old sweats' rifle drill did not present much difficulty, after a few times 'climbing' up and down the weapon, but to the novice there was need for longer practice. This, at any rate, enabled the sergeant-major to revive his last war verbal accomplishments.

BOMB THROWING

No. 36

XERCISE

MAP READING

Firing on the range gave to all a sense of military importance. To some, the old technique of sight and squeeze returned without much trouble, except that caused by an unsteady position, the consequence of a rounded girth. But the overall efficiency of the Home Guard increased, in spite of the jests of music-hall comedians.

Bombs came along to be studied and thrown – various types of bombs, Sticky, No. 36's, and others. They all provided scope for keenness and for some fun. Machine-carbines, machine-guns, tommy-guns, mortars and even guns. All these necessitated courses of instruction, endless practices on Sunday mornings, until the day came for firing blank or 'live'. Sometimes in the stripping and assembly of the weapons, parts would be dispensed with (or more truthfully, left out), and the comments of the 'class' upon such errors were not always helpful to the assembler. At any rate, to create a bang upon the range with any weapons was some symptom of usefulness to the perpetrator of the noise.

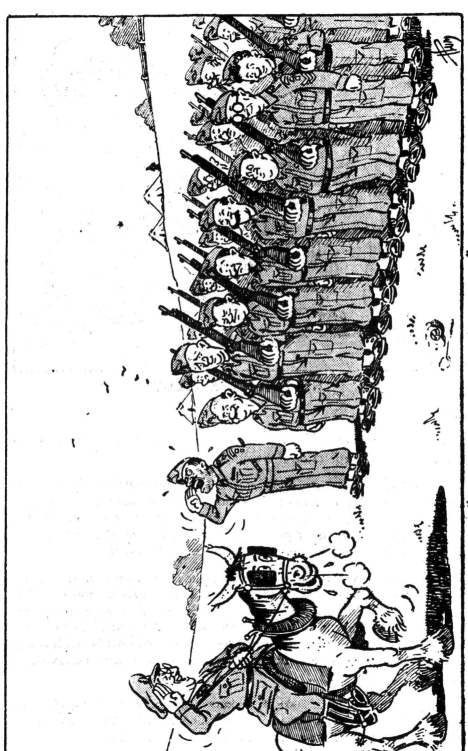

"PLATOONS WERE FORMED"

THE WIRELESS ISSUE

At the Headquarters of platoons and companies – mostly sited strategically near houses of 'local' importance – much planning went on. Exercises were framed to teach some salient part of military art; they undoubtedly did. Yet more especially, they brought out the renowned British habit of adaptation and the gift for improvising, including language.

Guerrilla warfare was the main study of the Home Guard for many days. Indeed it remained the basic tactics in scattered rural areas. How erstwhile immaculate fellows revelled in muddy contortions when approaching the 'enemy'! Crawling is an essential attribute of the soldier, but ofttimes the necessary compression of the middle portion could not be achieved in the H.G. exercises – and the buttocks proved conspicuous betrayers of presence!

Umpires had difficult tasks in making some participants in exercises understand that they were 'dead' or 'casualties'. Often the 'dead' arose and the 'casualties' walked, when the umpire turned away.

DON R'S HAVE THEIR USES

THE INTELLIGENCE SECTION

Night patrols and exercises would give scope for challenge and password, but often other things were said too. 'Prisoners' taken stood a poor chance of escaping; guards were pretty careful that way. Specialist sections became necessary as the Home Guard progressed. Signallers were trained in the art of flag-wagging and dotting-and-dashing with lamps. They learned the way to send and receive messages, lay lines and speak in weird phonetics on telephones. Even between the strict and precise 'battle' messages, some humour would intrude. Later on, wireless was issued, and this proved to be a never-failing source of interest to all concerned, including the public.

Eventually motor bicycles came along and soon dispatch riders were fitted on them. It was a thrilling part these fellows played in exercises, and on occasion they learned, at their destinations, that they had ridden rough-shod over bridges that had been 'blown up' and even through areas held by the 'enemy'.

With the formation of Intelligence Sections, there was a concentration upon map reading. To acquire this knowledge was not difficult when maps became more plentiful, yet to the end, some found that the spot on the map did not correspond with the one on the ground – when they got there! Prismatic compasses, 25-years-old, were found among the last war relics, but often the way to use them had grown pretty dim. 'Do you add to or subtract from Magnetic North to get True North?' That was usually the first try-out in the quest to re-discover knowledge. Intelligence had a hectic time in the hurly-burly of exercise, but in quieter spells they managed to see the lighter side and even answer some rude comments from a distance.

DIGGING REQUIRES STRONG (ARMY) BOOTS

THE
SAME
OLD
STORY

— BUT THE
SAME OLD
ENDING

ACK ACK

When some of the Home Guard personnel had to be transferred to Anti-Aircraft batteries, a new chapter was opened. Those who joined the 'Ack-Acks' were given a flash of scarlet, and this served to increase their prestige. As time wore on, the demands of this service became heavy and towards the end many thousands helped in the defence of the homeland.

Units had to contact neighbouring battalions, become acquainted with the terrain of these battalions, their strengths and dispositions. Thus was born liaison. Many were the inter-changes between flanking units, invariably cemented by a more-than-passing friendship.

Between times, tactics progressed to a high standard and often surprises were sprung, as opposing forces attempted to bring off a 'fast one' against each other. Camouflage was widely practised, but in the early days (like King Alfred's cakes) the art was overdone. Sometimes 'Battlefields' included both fields and houses – and it was no uncommon sight to see walking trees in

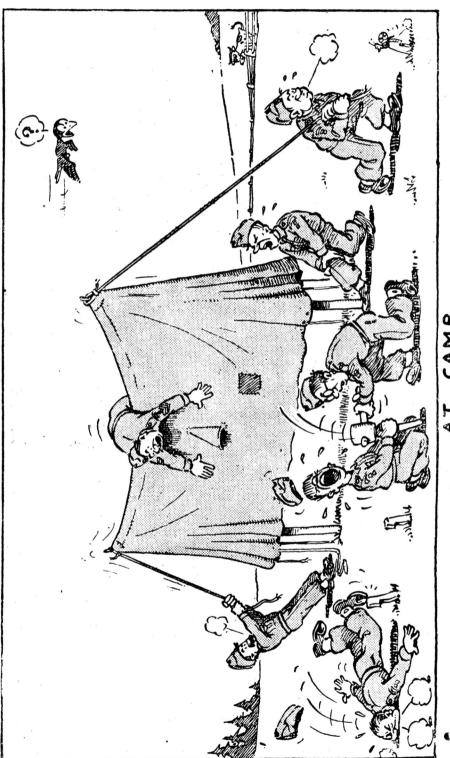

AT CAMP

CAMOUFLAGE

ROCKETEERS

a built-up area. This was remedied in later days. Often, too, the blacking of faces at night must have severely strained the domestic supply of boot polish – unless it was soot that was used.

Camps provided opportunity for hard work and hard play. The merry banter seeped through all restraints and schemes; it defied the weather and every hard patch; usually it came to its height in the sing-song at the canteen, when songs flowed with the beer (while it lasted).

Proficiency tests gave many an opportunity to show their prowess. It was interesting to observe the reactions of each candidate. Some were nervous (usually they did well when encouraged); some didn't care – anything; some talked a lot and knew little; some would try to argue it out if an answer were unacceptable to the examiner.

Home Guard Cadets were formed to give a necessary pre-training to the Youth of the country. Khaki once more proved a magnet. It was no unusual thing to have all the male occupants of the house in uniform. The youngsters were very keen, and with virile leadership, they went ahead. Many were the words

BATTLE INOCULATION

PROFICIENCY TEST

of advice given by fathers to sons. Such advice was imparted with appropriate solemnity as from an expert to the tyro. The effect was often the reverse of that expected and sometimes the quick promotion of the youngster destroyed any parental assumption of superiority!

Mention should be made to the First Aid Section. They attended courses of instruction, usually held by the M.O. of the Company. Their competence was revealed by the number of Ambulance badges earned. In the stress of training there were naturally accidents and at such times it was comforting to have First Aid men giving their efficient attention to cases. During exercises they had plenty of practice in the art of bandaging the 'wounded', also in stretcher-bearing. Now and again a 'casualty' did not want to be out of the 'battle', while others saw no hardship in being carried comfortably to some distant spot and thence by Ambulance to a Casualty Station.

But Home Guard days are now ended! The anticipated Stand-down order came when the crisis in which the force was born had disappeared. It faded out, well mustered, on its final parade – the rattle of drums and the speeches of notables. It gave up the weapons, gathered over four-and-a-half years' service, received certificates, and ended as it began, with spirit as its outstanding factor.

And now the alibis which served so well during training are invalid, but the art of improvising was long nurtured in the Home Guard, and maybe the old 'reasons' for a gentle 'local' crawl have been skilfully replaced by other acceptable 'stories'. Whatever happens, the humour which seeped through every hard circumstance will be remembered long after grim days have been dimmed by Time.

In humour, in keenness, in spirit, the Home Guard came true to type.

PARENTAL DISCIPLINE?

PROVIDING AN ALIBI

THE END

In May, 1945, came Victory in Europe and it has been revealed how grave was our plight in the 'Dunkirk' days. To what extent the Home Guard contributed to ultimate victory cannot be really assessed, but it did contribute by its watchful determination and its mighty numbers. It was ready to do its part had the occasion arisen; than that there could have been no greater praise. It would have tried valiantly and – we believe – succeeded in its task. Many thousands of our soldiers had their initial training in the Home Guard and to them, as to those who 'Stood Down', this booklet should help in the recounting of days that will speedily grow distant.